GW00659940

The Beauty of
NGORONGORO

Graham Mercer

Photographs by
Mohamed Amin, Duncan Willetts and Debbie Gaiger

Camerapix Publishers International
NAIROBI

First published 1993 by
Camerapix Publishers International,
P. O. Box 45048,
Nairobi,
Kenya

© Camerapix 1993

ISBN 1 874041 46 6

This book was designed and produced by
Camerapix Publishers International
P. O. Box 45048, Nairobi, Kenya

Edited by Jan Hemsing and Barbara Lawrance
Production Editor: Debbie Gaiger
Design: Kimberly Davis

All rights reserved. No part of this publication may be reproduced, stored in a retrieval
system, or transmitted in any form, or by any means, electronic, mechanical,
photocopying, recording or otherwise without permission in writing from Camerapix
Publishers International.

Printed in Hong Kong by South China Printing Co.

Half-title: Bull elephant grazing on lush scrub beneath the Crater wall.
*Title pages: Blush of flamingo reflected in the still waters of Lake Makat (also
known as Magadi).*
Contents: Rhino and calf — rare survivors in the battle against extinction.
*Following pages: Colourful flowers frame the verdant beauty of Ngorongoro
Crater.*

Contents

1. Introduction: Creation of Ngorongoro

In 1923 a young Scotsman, appropriately named Hunter, camped in Ngorongoro Crater, as a guide and professional hunter to two American clients. Their safari, one of the first organized tours of this now world-famous sanctuary, gives some idea of the relative remoteness of the Crater and the Serengeti in those days, for the journey from Arusha to Tabora, via the Crater and the Serengeti, was made entirely on foot and took ninety days.

Whilst in Ngorongoro, Hunter had paid a visit to a dilapidated farmhouse on the hillwash of the Crater wall, between the wall itself and the Lerai Forest, and almost directly below the site of the present Crater and Wildlife lodges which stand on the Crater rim. The neglected farm contained little but a pack of equally neglected Australian kangaroo hounds. Their master, Captain G.H.R. (George) Hurst, had moved into Ngorongoro as a rancher soon after the First World War, hoping to persuade the Custodian of Enemy Property to let him buy a farm on the far side of the Crater, appropriated from its German owner. His dream of living out his life in that wild and glorious arena was brought to a very tragic end, for his application for legal ownership was turned down in favour of Sir Charles Ross. Hurst, perhaps to alleviate his disappointment, set off on a hunting safari and was killed by an elephant at Kilwa, on the Tanganyika coast.

It was at about this time that Hunter came across the starving hounds, shot some small game for them to eat and, a little later, returned to find them 'in excellent shape'. He went out into the Crater and with their help . . . 'collected five good lions, knowing that their hides would bring a good price in

Opposite: One of East Africa's smallest antelopes — Kirk's dik-dik, shy denizen of the bush.

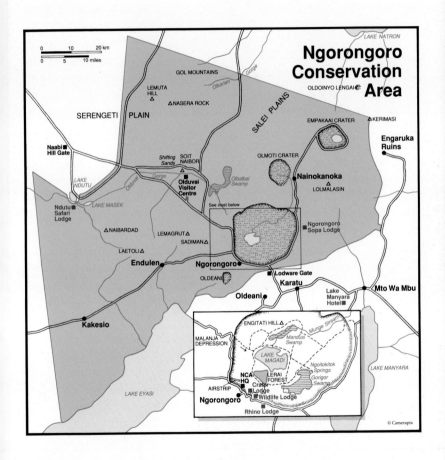

Ngorongoro Conservation Area

LAKE NATRON

GOL MOUNTAINS

Olkarien Gorge

LEMUTA HILL

△ NASERA ROCK

OLDOINYO LENGAI

SERENGETI PLAIN

SALEI PLAINS

EMPAKAAI CRATER

△ KERIMASI

Engaruka Ruins

Naabi ■ Hill Gate

Shifting Sands

SOIT NAIBOR

OLMOTI CRATER

Nainokanoka

LAKE NDUTU

Olduvai Visitor Centre

Olbalbal Swamp

△ LOLMALASIN

Olduvai Gorge

LAKE MASEK

See inset below

Ndutu Safari Lodge

△ NAIBARDAD

LEMAGRUT △

Ngorongoro Sopa Lodge

SADIMAN △

LAETOLI △

Endulen

Ngorongoro

Lodware Gate

OLDEANI

Karatu

Oldeani

Lake Manyara Hotel ■

Mto Wa Mbu

Kakesio

0   10   20 km
0   5   10 miles

Inset (See inset below)

ENGITATI HILL △

Munge Stream

MALANJA DEPRESSION

Mandusi Swamp

LAKE MAGADI

Ngoitokitok Springs

Gorigor Swamp

LAKE MANYARA

NCA HQ

LERAI FOREST

AIRSTRIP

Crater Lodge

Ngorongoro

Wildlife Lodge

Rhino Lodge

LAKE EYASI

© Camerapix

11

Nairobi. It never occurred to me that the day would come when lions would be carefully protected as a game animal. . . '

The farmhouse still stands, and so do the ruins of the farm which the ill-fated Hurst had hoped to buy, across the Crater floor by the Munge River, and it might be appropriate here, before describing the physical beauty of Ngorongoro, to talk a little more about its past. For history has a beauty of its own. As they drive around the Crater, few tourists will be aware that they are driving through time as well as space.

When such tourists stop for drinks at the picnic spot at the edge of the Lerai, excited by the morning's or evening's recent game viewing, they are little more than a stone's throw from that 'haunted' farm. Among the spirits which reside there may be that of Friedrich Wilhelm Siedentopf, who actually built the house before the Great War. His brother Adolph had, like Captain Hurst later, entered the Crater as a squatter, around 1899. Adolph established the farm by the Munge River and received title to the land just before the war. Friedrich's property was never legally recognized.

What kind of lives must those two brothers, one at either side of that magnificent caldera, have lived? What thoughts and dreams possessed them? Did they visit each other regularly — or not at all? Did they receive visits from other Europeans? Were their lonely nights made less so by dreams of frauleins with flaxen-hair or by the soft realities of Maasai concubines? Or did they merely enjoy their splendid isolation?

They could never have imagined that within a lifetime's span their wild and private world would be invaded by thousands of tourists, eagerly photographing the lions which the Siedentopfs (and Hunter) would have shot as vermin. Nor would they have imagined that one day the Maasai would be

obliged to leave their old pastures. And surely they could never have foreseen that in the much shorter term they themselves, with their own herds, would be forced out. But war with its swaggering stupidity reached out and wrecked the lives of those who only wished to be left alone. The Siedentopf brothers were in the right place at the wrong time and, by the end of 1916, had lost everything and were gone.

Another German name which figures significantly in the modern history of Ngorongoro is that of Dr Oscar Baumann, the first recorded overseas visitor to the Crater. Baumann first looked down upon 'the oblong bowl of Ngorongoro' (as he prosaically describes that enchanting scene) at noon on 18 March, 1892. He wasn't a man to let the grass grow under his feet and was soon camping on the floor of the Crater — or what, more properly, is a caldera, or collapsed crater. It was, he writes, 'alive with a great number of game'.

This overwhelming array of animals had now, as it happens, been augmented by a rather exotic newcomer, an Arabian camel — but not for long, as the poor beast (hardly surprisingly) keeled over with a bad cough and never recovered. Its driver, Mohammed, became depressed and, according to Baumann, lost weight, but the party pressed on, minus the camel, to the south of the swampy country by Koitoktok Springs and on to the 'pleasant acacia forest' of Lerai. Their route out of the Crater must have taken them across, or very close to, the exact spot where Friedrich Siedentopf would one day build his farm.

All this is very recent history by Ngorongoro's age-embracing standards. Although the Crater itself is a relatively new arrival in geological terms, it is merely the jewel in a most astonishing crown, for the Conservation Area as a whole

Above: Written in the eroded strata of Olduvai Gorge is the story of early man, vital clues to our own beginnings.

Opposite: Stone tools found at Olduvai on display in the onsite museum.

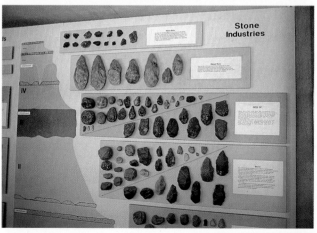

15

extends for over 8,320 sq km, representing, incidentally, a unique experiment in multiple land use. And a little to the north-west of the Crater, history has been demonstrably laid bare, for there the short-grass plains are riven by a rock-strewn gully, the famous Olduvai Gorge, which has yielded, among more important finds, a horde of stone tools dating from the beginning of the Lower to the Middle and Upper Pleistocene.

Olduvai — a corruption of *oldupai*, the Maasai name for the wild sisal (*Sanseviera robusta*) which grows profusely in the gorge — is yet another of Ngorongoro's infinite variety of wonders. Like the Crater itself it has an interesting recent history as well as a more engrossing distant past, for its archaeological significance was stumbled upon (almost literally) by an engagingly entitled German, one Professor Kattwinkel, when in hot pursuit of a butterfly in 1911.

Kattwinkel took back with him to Berlin some fossil bones which he collected in the gorge, including those of 'a three-toed horse'. They were received in Germany with such interest that, with the support of no less a personage than the Kaiser himself, an expedition was sent out in 1913 led by the eminent geologist Professor Hans Reck.

Amongst Reck's findings at Olduvai was a human skeleton estimated to be of the Middle Pleistocene era. Unfortunately for Germany, proposals to follow up Reck's discoveries with four further expeditions in 1914 had to be abandoned with the declaration of the 1914-1918 war.

It was to be twenty years after Kattwinkel's surprisingly rewarding butterfly-catching adventure, however, that the true importance of the gorge began to be revealed, for in 1931 a man whose name was to become as well known as Olduvai itself arrived to subject its layers of history and pre-history to his intelligent and single-minded scrutiny. He was, of course, Dr Louis Leakey. Initially Dr Leakey found stone tools, but for him, his wife Mary and later his sons Jonathan and Richard, these were only the first scattered pieces of a most intriguing chronological jigsaw puzzle, the implications of which were to be important to all mankind, for even in the partial completing of that complex puzzle we have seen ourselves, revealed across the better part of two million years, in our anthropological childhood. Or someone pretty much like us.

After the simple tools, bones and skulls of giant sheep with horns of six foot spread, and pigs as big as hippos were unearthed. But more exciting still were the bones and skulls of Ancient Man (or near-Man), the hominids *Australopithecus boisei* — 'Nutcracker man' as the Leakeys named him — and the smaller, more delicate *Homo habilis*, a creature with a larger brain and the ability, it would seem, to fashion tools and use them.

The gorge in itself is not a beautiful place, but there is an aesthetic sublimity in the heavily charged silence of its primeval past, the history of which is written in the earth itself, in the five distinct and subtle-shaded bands of clay and sand which rise in layers from their bed of lava to form the sixty-metre (200-foot) wall of Olduvai's main sector. Some forty kilometres (twenty-five miles) south of this geological history book Mary Leakey discovered, in the petrified ash of a volcano, the footprints of hominids, animals and birds. The footprints suggest that the hominids were striding out in much the same manner as we might do ourselves, but that stroll through the falling ash of Satiman took place some three-and-a-half million years ago.

Such scenes bring the contemplative visitor face to face at

17

last with the creator of Ngorongoro and its beauty, for the beds of lava and the gently drifting ash which speak on an ancient theme were the work of an ancient God. To best appreciate the wonder of his work it is suggested that you find an unobstructed viewpoint on the southern rim of the Crater, in the area of the tourist lodges — or better still on the terrace of one of them, preferably with a drink in your hand (perhaps a hot one, for the average altitude at the rim is 2,316 metres [7,600 feet]. These heights were known to the Germans as the 'Winter Highlands' and the air, inside and outside the Crater, can be cold and damp).

Assuming that the air is also clear, the observer can look out across this great and famous bowl of savannah grass with its steep, 610-metre (2,000-foot) walls and gentle mounds, its small acacia forest and the adjacent lake, hazily polished like a misted mirror and framed by broad white soda flats. In the distance, to the north-east and beyond the Crater, stands Lolmalasin, and curving anti-clockwise around the caldera from this 3,657-metre (12,000-foot) peak stand the mountains Sirua, Olmoti, Makarut and finally Oldeani. Behind Sirua and Lolmalasin rise Empakaai and Kerimasi, and a little further into the distance the sharper cone of the active volcano Lengai, the Mountain of God. All approach or exceed 2,743 metres (9,000 feet). It is a gloriously weathered volcanic country of rounded curves and great sweeps and swells of muted greens and browns, moulded from the liquid rock and modified by time.

According to geologists, Ngorongoro rose from the basalt-flooded floor of an earlier rift, when the fluent lavas ceased to issue from the central, elongated cracks and forced their increasingly viscous way through seven new and individual

vents. The thicker lava cooled rapidly into great domes, thus creating Ngorongoro and its attendant peaks. But what the Gods create they also destroy and, in this department of destruction, the God Vulcan — for it is his work you stand and admire — comes into his own. The fault that caused the Rift Valley sheared off the eastern edges of the newly-made highlands and the mountain peaks were blasted into the troposphere by frustrated underground gases. The high remaining walls of Ngorongoro, Empakaai, and Olmoti collapsed into their caldera and, from such chaos, evolved the spacious softness and serenity — and the genuine beauty — which one sees from the comfort of the lodges on the Crater's edge.

The Crater floor is more or less circular and about fourteen kilometres (nine miles) in diameter. It is fairly flat and the grasses which predominate are mown into short submission by the scything incisors of tens of thousands of herbivores. But the apparent flatness and smoothness is broken in places by a variety of features. The wall of the Crater itself is in fact a circular fault from which molten material once welled. As this flow cooled and became covered in vegetation it formed the bumpy falls of land that can be seen under Crater View in the south and behind the ruins of the old Siedentopf farm in the north. These knolls are known to the Maasai as Nolkaria, the 'Hills of the Red Earth'.

Kitati Hill, again in the north, seems flat-topped but is in fact a defunct and miniature volcano with its own shallow crater. Its Maasai name means 'Girdle', of the type worn by their women, as the hill is circular in shape, with abrupt sides. To the west of the Lerai Forest lie piles of rock which were swept into the Crater when a lake by the rim emptied itself through a

Left: Herd of elephant make their way across the Crater floor. Normally, only bulls graze inside the Crater — cows and calves preferring to browse the forest thickets higher up.

sudden breach in the wall, a phenomenon known to geologists as 'lahar'. The Maasai, more figuratively, call the jumble of boulders 'Kung'— 'The Kneecaps'.

The Lerai was also named by the Maasai, after the yellow-bark acacias of which the forest is composed. The *Acacia xanthophloea*, to give the yellow-barks the dignity of their specific name — from the Greek *xanthos* (yellow) and *phloos* (bark or skin) — are lovely trees, despite their not-so-lovely former reputation. Before the cause of malaria was known, the yellow-bark was declared guilty by association and nicknamed the 'Fever Tree', its watery habitat being equally attractive to the female anopheles mosquito — the malaria bearer.

The forest might not promote death but it certainly harbours it, for the Lerai is littered with dead wood, the result of natural ageing, elephant damage and also flooding, for though the acacia thrive near water they cannot tolerate too much of it.

Give a tree a bad name and it doesn't necessarily stick: its old name is rarely heard now and it seems unlikely that anyone really believed that a tree could actually transmit malaria. Perhaps the colour of its bark, which inspired normally objective botanists to use adjectives such as 'evil', 'pallid', 'leprous', 'sickly', and 'sinister', landed the acacia with the less pleasant of its popular names. Many people, however, find the colour — streaked with purple-brown where the beautifully smooth bark has peeled or been stripped, and viewed in bright light and in the context of the overall delicacy of the trees — quite attractive. Nor are they only appealing to humans. For practical rather than aesthetic reasons, they are much favoured by lions as convenient scratch-pads. Habitual claw-sharpening on their trunks can leave the trees deeply but

impressively scarred for life. Less destructively, countless birds make the yellow-barks their home, particularly the weaver birds whose nests sway precariously from their branches in the wind.

Adjacent to the north-east corner of the Lerai Forest is Lake Makat and, beyond the lake, Mundusi Swamp, stretching away beneath Kitati Hill to the foot of the rising land to the north, and fed by the narrow Munge River which skirts the ruined farm. Makat is alkaline (it is commonly known by its Kiswahili name Magadi, which means 'soda') and attracts flamingos. It also attracts Maasai, who still bring their herds, under permit (or sometimes illicitly) down the age-old trails, so that the cattle can lick the salt-rich margins of the lake and drink from the freshwater streams which filter down from the walls. (These streams, incidentally, provide year-round sustenance for the Crater's resident wildlife, whereas the wildebeest and zebra in the nearby Serengeti are obliged to follow the rains to find fresh pasture).

Right: Lengthening shadows silhouette an Acacia thorn tree against the azure blue of a late Ngorongoro Crater afternoon.

2. The Proud and Colourful Pastoralists

The Maasai, those proud and colourful pastoralists, were 'persuaded' to leave the Serengeti and Ngorongoro by the end of 1958 and to sign a treaty which reads like many such treaties. It recalls the 'agreements' made between the US government and the North American Indians in the previous century. Between the stolid lines of officialdom one can read the unwritten, unarticulated responses of the Maasai themselves, eloquent silences heavy with dignity and sadness; 'We, the Laigwanak of the Loliondo Divisions of the Masai District . . . understand that as a result of this renunciation we shall not be entitled . . . in the years to come . . . to reside in or use in future the land . . . which we have habitually used in the past. We agree to move ourselves, our possessions, our cattle and all our other animals out of this land by the advent of the next short rains . . . '

And so the Loliondo Maasai lost their fabulous 'Siringet' — 'The Great Open Place' and the Crater whose name, it is said, was bestowed not by them but by the Kalenjin, although its origins are disputed. The clink of cowbells in the cold caldera morning was of the past and the pastures tremble now to the tread of heavy tyres as well as hooves, and the hooves are wild. The 'advent of the next short rains' brought a sweet greenness to the plains but a bitterness, no doubt, to many Maasai hearts.

The Maasai, as always, have learned to live with change, without changing. It is their weakness, their strength and their glory and, without them, the beauty of the Ngorongoro experience would be diminished. They still have access to the slopes and plains around and beyond the Crater, outside the Serengeti, and their herds of hump-backed cattle may sometimes be seen grazing alongside zebra or wildebeest, a

harmony reflected in the Maasai's own ability to live, unlike so many of us, at one with their environment. The people, generally fine-featured and cheerfully hospitable, wrapped in red-brown *shukas* or blankets, the womenfolk bedecked with beads and bangles and easily-induced smiles, are seen wherever the grazing is good and the law allows.

It is difficult to determine the success or failure of the Ngorongoro Conservation Unit as an experiment in multiple land use, for the interests of pastoralists, farmers, foresters and conservationists have obvious incompatibilities. There is no difficulty at all in recognizing the success of the Crater, for its value to Tanzania in material terms, and to the world for its own sake, is almost self-evident. Yet sometimes, when gazing down into that splendid natural bowl, it is difficult not to spare a thought for the Loliondo Maasai, who were moved out so that our own strange tribes, bedecked with cameras rather than beads, could move in.

A sincere but sentimental thought, for the Maasai were themselves outsiders, and are relative newcomers to the Crater, probably arriving in the area during the first half of the nineteenth century but certainly well established when Baumann passed through in 1892. According to Maasai folklore, fierce battles were fought in the vicinity of the Crater Highlands, against an enemy traditionally known as *il Adoru* — possibly a clan of the uncompromising Tatog, another Nilo-Hamitic tribe associated with Ngorongoro. The Tatog almost certainly lived in the caldera at one time, though this is denied by the Maasai. Henry Fosbrooke, one-time head of the Conservation Unit and the author of the richly informative book *Ngorongoro: The Eighth Wonder*, confirms that the Tatog

Opposite: Maasai herdsmen and youngsters tend cattle at a salt lick on their old pastures in the Crater.

Below: Maasai cattle graze dusty Crater floor close to wildebeest and zebra.

'used to come back to the Crater and perform religious ceremonies at certain sacred trees'.

A section the tribe still lives by Lake Eyasi, on the southern borders of the Conservation Unit, though the largest group of Tatog, known as the Barabaig, is centred upon Mount Hanang, a 3,657-metre (12,000-foot) extinct volcano a little way to the south-west. They are a most interesting people but like the Maasai (to whom they were an implacable but much respected enemy) they are not averse, when aroused or offended, to the occasional show of violent force.

Also by Lake Eyasi lives a tribe with a less pugnacious though no less interesting reputation, the Hadza, who number only a few hundred and who still practise hunting — using two-metre (six-and-a-half-foot) longbows — and gathering. Like the bushmen of southern Africa they smoke tubular stone pipes and speak a click language, though the Hadza are much larger in physique and darker in complexion, and attempts to link the two tongues or cultures have so far failed.

In the rough triangle formed by Lake Eyasi, the Crater and Lake Manyara live a very different group of people, known in Kiswahili as the Mbulu but more properly called the Iraqw. The Iraqw only moved into the Crater Highlands after the First World War, when their tribal lands to the south were becoming overcrowded. After the War, dispossessed German farmers were allowed to re-settle, though not on their former lands, and were obliged to break new soil (and perhaps old backs and hearts) out on the plateau above the western wall of the Rift.

This plateau is a pleasant, rolling country which travellers from the south and east pass through after climbing up from Mto Wa Mbu en route to the Crater. Beyond the edge of the

escarpment the road continues to rise gradually, and then assumes an irregular rhythm of gentle undulations across the Mbulu Plateau, before beginning the steeper ascent of Ngorongoro itself. This fertile tableland, where brown-furrowed fields and pallid sweeps of wheat and maize stretch out beneath the darker forests of the highlands, was surprisingly uninhabited before 1918.

On being allowed to resettle at the War's end, some of the reinstated German farmers set up home on the lower slopes of Oldeani Mountain to the south-west of the Crater and planted coffee. In doing so they attracted the attention of the Iraqw, who initially came to work the German-owned farms but who soon began to settle the adjoining country in their own right. When Hitler's armies were marching into the Sudetenland in 1938 the Iraqw were annexing, with more legality and less aggression, the plateau beneath the Crater Highlands, while the poor German farmers, their hard-won lands again appropriated, were rounded up once more and interned.

A Wheat Scheme was organized to help fill the stomachs upon which armies are supposed to march, but this time it was the Iraqw whose land was sacrificed to the Allied cause. The British government promised to return it to them after the war and, perhaps to everyone's surprise, actually did so. Now the Iraqw, wrapped in blankets against the cool winds of the plateau, stroll along the tracks between the settlements or work the rich red loam, under the heights of Ngorongoro and Oldeani, the 'Mountain of Bamboos'.

Traditionally they were mainly cattle breeders, but not as exclusively as the Maasai, and the cultivation of crops (maize, beans, sorghum, millet, eleusine and sweet potatoes) is a long established feature of their lifestyle. Being enterprising and

Above: Newly circumcised female Maasai initiates and their young sisters pose on the rim of the Ngorongoro Crater.

Left: Smiling girl initiate in decorative and symbolic make-up.

Opposite: Traditional bead necklaces of the Maasai add their own splash of colour to the beauty of Ngorongoro.

industrious people they have, since moving to the plateau, adapted themselves to crop growing on a larger scale and, within decades, have made the jump from wooden hoes (used as late as the 1950s) to sophisticated tractors.

Of all the tribes associated with Ngorongoro, the oldest surviving people of the Highlands (of Kenya as well as the Crater) are said to be the Dorobo, known in Kiswahili as Wandorobo and to themselves as Okiek. They are also, with the possible exception of the Hadza and the Sandawe, the true remaining aborigines of Kenya and northern Tanzania, though no one can be sure. What is certain is that the Dorobo, in common with so many aboriginal people throughout the world, have been treated as inferiors and pushed aside (as recently as the end of the nineteenth century) by more aggressive and 'advanced' intruders.

A missionary map of 1848, showing the lands beyond Kilimanjaro as inhabited by Dorobo, describes them as 'a very poor people despised and maltreated by all tribes around'. The plural form of their Kiswahili name, Wandorobo, is the same as that for tsetse flies, though there is nothing to suggest that the epithet is intentionally demeaning. To the Maasai, for whom they work as smiths, circumcisers, rainmakers and attendants of the dead, they are Il Torrobo, 'poor men — men without cattle' and decidely lower caste.

And yet the Dorobo, of all the tribes which have lived in or around the Crater, perhaps come nearest to its quintessential spirit, even more so than the Maasai, for the Dorobo are truly of the wild, creatures of the forest as much as the leopard and the duiker and the bushbuck, and like them — more shadow, it sometimes seems, than substance — vague beings who drift through a vaguer world, somewhere between abstraction and

reality. More than one book written by the old hunters and game wardens of Kenya endorsed the bushcraft of these little men of the forest who, it was widely acclaimed, could follow tracks which no one else could see and tell, from listening to the very breathing of an animal lying up in thick bush, how far away it was and whether it was a buffalo or rhino.

It is easy to romanticize Africa and those of its people who most satisfy our craving for the exotic and the captivating, but it is difficult, for those who know and love the bush, not to feel some affinity with the Dorobo. Esteemed as gunbearers and trackers, and as hunters and trappers in their own right, whose love of game meat and deep reverence for honey kept them so close to nature that they were themselves an inseparable part of it, the Wandorobo lived almost entirely on and among the creatures of the wild. Their only concessions to domesticity were the keeping of dogs and bees, and these only to further their hunter-gatherer instincts.

Where the Maasai have an almost worshipful regard for their God-given cattle and will talk of them for hours, the Dorobo talk of the animals of the forest. Their simple beliefs are expressed in a summarized and rare insight into the Dorobo mind, recorded by one of the few authorities on the tribe, Dr Huntingford. The voice is that of a Dorobo.

'The Dorobo know the spoor of all the animals, they see the animals that other people never see, the animals are their neighbours with whom they share the forest. Animals are only a little different from people, they too have cunning, they are not bad. We eat some of them and some of them eat us.'

The Dorobo, the Okiek, driven into the highland forests of what is now Kenya and to a smaller extent northern Tanzania by the more ambitious and powerful Kikuyu, Nandi and

Above: Maasai herdsman rests amid sere grasses in the Ngorongoro Highlands while waiting for the dry season to end.

Opposite: Future warriors learn responsibility early in life as cattle herders.

Maasai (not to mention the white tribes from the west) still move among the great indigenous trees of the Mau and the Mathews Range but, like the forests themselves, are diminishing, so that their many clans are isolated and might number, in total, less than ten thousand individuals. Even these, adopting the language and customs of the peoples with whom they associate, are gradually losing their tribal identity.

There were still Dorobo in the Crater in 1892 for, on 21 March, Baumann's caravan passed one of their camps, 'the surrounding of which was littered by game refuse, over which ravens, marabus and vultures were fighting'. The hunter gatherers were obviously living in peace, if not in harmony, with the pastoral Maasai, for a Maasai enclosure — a warrior *enkang* or family manyatta — was close by. Baumann camped in the Lerai that night and a tragic and curious incident took place when, having been forewarned by Dorobo that the Maasai were about to attack, some of Baumann's men fired on approaching figures in the darkness.

The following morning the explorer was horrified to find two emaciated corpses outside his camp. Beside them was a starving old man who fearlessly cursed the German. 'You wallow in milk and meat', he cried, 'and shoot at us, who are dying of hunger'. He was given meat which he swallowed raw (as some Maasai still do). Baumann had written, the previous day, that the Maasai in the Crater were in such a plight that ' . . . dead donkeys were a delicacy for them: but they also devoured the skins, bones and even horns of cattle'.

Appalling famine was indeed sweeping the land and the closing decades of the nineteenth century were harrowing for the Maasai. Internecine battles had wrought destruction among the clans, a smallpox epidemic had ravaged them further, rinderpest had swept south from the Horn of Africa, wiping out cattle and game in their thousands, and a plague of locusts had destroyed the grazing. Baumann had written about whole districts of the Serengeti being depopulated, and yet the Crater was then, as it is now, a bowl of plenty. And some of the best hunters in the world, the Dorobo, subservient even to starving Maasai, were living alongside them.

The Maasai do not normally touch game meat, with the occasional exception of buffalo and eland, which resemble cattle, but according to Baumann they were now, in their desperation, spearing wildebeest and rhino. Either they were not very good at it or the 'starvelings' which Baumann refers to had recently moved in from the Serengeti as refugees, and had not had time to build up their strength. Whatever the case, while 'terrific herds of game were roaming in the wide plains' of Ngorongoro, there were Maasai women 'reduced to walking skeletons', 'children resembling deformed frogs' and 'warriors who could hardly crawl on all fours'.

Scarcely paradise, yet had the starving Maasai mused upon their wretchedness, an awful irony might have struck them, for the Maasai equivalent of the 'Garden of Eden' was also a place shared by the Il Parakwo, ancestors of the Maasai, and the Il Torrobo, ancestors of the Dorobo, all children of the Eve-like figure Naiteru-Kop, who doted upon the moon and by so doing condemned her descendents to mortality. The Il Parakwo were God's chosen people and received, via a string connected to the earth, cattle from heaven, while the Dorobo had to hunt for their food. A jealous Dorobo hunter cut the string and God (Enkai), in anger at their lack of watchfulness, turned on the Il Parakwo and condemned them to a life of famine and a struggle to fight for their cattle.

41

3. Garden of Eden

The moon survives and shines down, sometimes most enchantingly, into that other Garden of Eden known to the world as Ngorongoro Crater. The Maasai and the Dorobo, the English and the German squatters and settlers and the stone-age people and all who went before them have left the Crater for pastures new, or for another kind of paradise. The Garden of Eden is now 'drive-in' only, and the travellers and tourists and wildlife enthusiasts are its inheritors.

What brings them here? Not history nor ethnology, absorbing as these are. Not even scenery, though in any other country of the world Ngorongoro would be outstanding for this alone. They come because there is nowhere else on this earth where they can see, in such ease and comfort, such a spectacular accumulation of wildlife in such a splendid and unique setting. They come, mostly, across the Great Rift and the Mbulu Plateau, finally climbing through the temperate evergreen forest and emerging at the Crater rim, to follow the track around its edge to their lodge or hostel or camping site.

The first view of the Crater is eagerly anticipated as travellers and tourists peer through the screen of trees along the rim to catch a glimpse of what, in so many cases, they have come so far to see. That first view is exciting but incomplete. When the full panorama is visible, usually from one of the hotels on the rim, it may not take the breath away but it can cause newcomers to look down upon it in speechless wonder.

There are greater thrills ahead, when the descent into the caldera is made. Meanwhile there is much to see along the rim itself, and many tourists are taken aback when they stroll around the gardens of their lodge and find a wild buffalo grazing on the lawn, or see a large mongoose nosing among the trackside vegetation. This particular mongoose, the Large

Grey, is well named for it is over three feet long and — would you believe? — grey. It was venerated by the ancient Egyptians and is sometimes called the Egyptian mongoose. Almost entirely terrestrial, it is versatile in habit, being omnivorous and moving around by night as much as day.

There are larger predators around the Crater edge. Leopards, more adaptable and common than is often realized, are as much at home in the highland forests as they are in the lowland bush, and are occasionally sighted quite close to the lodges. Being largely solitary and nocturnal (though they are seen by daylight in many places) you would have to be very lucky to encounter one, but those who do get a reasonably close view are unlikely to forget it. If any animal can be said to possess charisma, the leopard does, with its disturbingly bewitching blend of beauty and controlled ferocity.

Its reputation for savagery was well-earned, but derives, in the main, from the days when it was widely hunted, and when leopard-skin coats were acceptably — and expensively — fashionable. If the occasional leopard raked gangrenous wounds into the flesh of some pursuing hunter, or disembowelled him, it is hardly the fault of the animal. Leopards just don't enjoy being smashed by bullets from a .375 magnum, and their tolerance of people who wish to part them prematurely from their beautiful coats is noticeably limited.

In fact the leopard has been much maligned. It is certainly capable of awe-inspiring viciousness when provoked or cornered, but females make very caring mothers, and leopards in general will rarely attack humans if left in peace. What they do attack, as their natural prey, are mammals up to the size of a reedbuck (including domestic stock) and birds up to the size

Above: Resting up during the day, Ngorongoro's leopards stalk stealthily through the Crater's forests by night.
Opposite top: Windsor Hotels' Crater Lodge stands atop the crater rim with stupendous views over the bowl of the Crater.
Opposite: Close-up of the action more than 460 metres (1,500 feet) below.

of storks, as well as certain reptiles or amphibians. They have catholic tastes but are said to have a predilection for young baboons, monkeys and domestic dogs, and there is evidence that jackals constitute a favourite element of their diet in the Crater.

Another cat which is found along the rim (and elsewhere) is the serval, smaller and relatively leggier than the leopard and with a conspicuously short tail. Its large-eared head is small compared with the body and its hind legs are longer than the fore. These apparently incongruous features might present a picture of an uncharacteristically awkward cat, but the serval, its tawny coat heavily spotted, is quite handsome and perfectly adapted to pouncing in a sharply parabolic leap on to a small rodent, among the long grasslands which it often favours, or springing almost vertically upwards to pluck birds from the air .

Birds are plentiful both in and outside the Crater, but along the partly forested rim there are some particularly resplendent varieties. Many pleasant hours may be passed in unrepentant indolence in the gardens or on the verandahs of the lodges, watching, among other species, Bronze and Taccazze sunbirds busy among the exotic blossoms. Both species are large by sunbird standards, the males attaining a length of eight-and-a-half inches including their central tail feathers, and both can appear black in poor light. In clear sunlight, however, the Bronze male is a shimmering bronze-green and its Taccazze counterpart (named after a river in northern Ethiopia) a scintillating metallic violet, its head glossed with a bronze or coppery sheen.

Other sunbirds are found wherever conditions are suitable, and where there is a plentiful supply of the particular nectars

or insects on which they frenziedly feed. They include the Variable, the Scarlet-chested, the Eastern Double-collared and the Long-tailed Golden-winged, the males of which are all as striking, in their tiny but brilliantly iridescent vitality, as their names suggest.

The vantage point of the rim, almost 610 metres (2,000 feet) above the caldera floor, sometimes offers the unusual opportunity of watching a soaring bird of prey, such as the Augur buzzard, from above, though bird and observer will look down through very different eyes. Diurnal birds of prey hunt predominantly by sight and have acutely developed vision. A buzzard's *fovea*, the sensitive depression in the *retina* of the eye, is said to contain 1,000,000 cones to the square millimetre, far more than the human eye, and the resolving power of the eyes of certain hawks and eagles is at least eight times that of our own. Such birds have stereoscopic vision, as we do, and are thus able to judge quickly changing distances with great accuracy as they swoop to kill.

Another bird of prey with excellent eyesight and which is sometimes seen from the Crater rim is the Egyptian vulture. Strangely for a vulture it is almost completely white, making it easy to identify on the ground (in flight its tail, shaped like an elongated diamond, is a distinguishing feature). It is small for its kind, like the darker Hooded vulture which is also found in the Crater and, when seen at close quarters, rather scruffy and unprepossessing. Egyptian vultures, sometimes known as 'Pharoah's chickens', are locally common in parts of Africa but in Tanzania are rarely found outside the north.

Their preferred diet is offal and excrement, which might explain why they are so often found around Maasai encampments and other 'natural' human settlements. They are

Above: Tawny eagle with prey.

Opposite: Rare sight in Ngorongoro Crater — a Ruppell's vulture. The birds find competition from other carnivores too great.

known to break open ostrich eggs by holding stones in their bills and using them as tools, an ingenious habit perhaps born out of desperation, for offal and excrement — even among vultures — cannot, surely, have a boundless appeal.

Taxonomically the Egyptian vulture is close to a remarkable bird called the lammergeyer, which is essentially a bird of the high mountains and towering cliffs. Nowadays classed with the vultures, it has a typical vulturine bill, scavenges, associates with pastoralists in Africa and visits refuse dumps outside Indian villages. Yet it remains a bird apart. Very few people know much about it and even their evidence sometimes conflicts, perhaps because of the variation in lammergeyer behaviour from one region to another.

The respected East African ornithologist John Williams says that lammergeyers are not gregarious and seldom approach animal carcases while other vultures are feeding. Salim Ali, the late and well-loved Indian bird expert, talks of them being commonly seen scavenging 'in company with griffons, neophrons, ravens and crows'. Ali also insists that the lammergeyer, ' . . . has never been known to attack live animals', but H.B. Cott, author of that marvellous book *Looking at Animals*, mentions accounts of these unusual birds 'knocking chamois, goats and klipspringers off cliffs and then following to feed on the mutilated corpse'.

They have also been known, he goes on, 'to pick up tortoises and drop them' (presumably deliberately and from a considerable height).

For the sake of the much-abused tortoise one must hope that he was misled, but circumstantial evidence offers little comfort, for it is well known that lammergeyers pick up large bones in a similar way and drop them to get at the marrow, for which purpose, it appears, evolution has provided them with an unusually long tongue.

The tortoises of Ngorongoro need not lose too much sleep, for lammergeyers are quite uncommon in East Africa, though from time to time they are seen in the Crater Highlands and other mountainous country. They can be recognized in flight by their distinctive silhouette, having long, narrow and angled wings and, like the Egyptian vulture, a tail shaped like an elongated diamond — though the lammergeyer is a much larger bird with a wingspan approaching three metres (ten feet).

4. Down into the Crater

There is, then, a great deal to see and do on and along the Crater rim, but nothing, not even a leopard or a lammergeyer, compares with the descent into the caldera and the exciting prospects, with respect to both landscape and wildlife, which await the traveller. Vehicles making this exciting journey go down into the Crater via the Seneto Road (a rather overstated title for a track which bears more resemblance to a fire escape hewn out of rock).

If, however, descending passengers ignore the vertiginous tumble of rock and vegetation just to their left, and the efficiency or otherwise of their vehicle's braking system, there is much to delight in — not least of which are the views, at certain points, into the distant caldera. Less phlegmatic travellers might prefer to direct their eyes and thoughts to their more immediate surroundings, in the hope of seeing a group of Mountain reedbuck (known as Chanler's reedbuck in East Africa) which live in this precipitous terrain. They are the smallest of the reedbuck and have, like the lammergeyer, an unusually wide and sporadic distribution — reflecting, no doubt, the isolated nature of their preferred habitats.

There are flowers, too, to admire in passing, and gorgeous butterflies, especially just after the rains, and the stark, Gothic beauty of the *Euphorbia kibwiensis*, succulent trees with crowns of upcurving green limbs, set on a cylindrical bole. The *Euphorbia* decorate the slopes like giant, over-ornate candelabra and, though their sap, a milky latex, is toxic like that of other members of the genus, their sinuous and flanged limbs, along their spiny tips, bear intricately pretty yellow flowers.

But all eyes are eventually drawn back to the Crater floor for, as the descent towards it eases, the real spectacle of

Ngorongoro begins to unfold, as the dark dots which lie scattered over the green or tawny plains resolve themselves into living creatures, perhaps twenty thousand or more in all, though numbers vary from season to season and year to year.

The most numerous of these is the wildebeest. There are so many that we tend to marvel at the herd and overlook the individual. Which is a pity, for the wildebeest, in its inimitable way, is an antelope worthy of our notice, however grotesque and comical it might appear to human eyes. The clichés about it being 'the clown of the plains' or having been 'designed by a committee' are appropriate enough, for the 'gnu' (now a little-used name of South African origin) often behaves in an apparently bizarre fashion and even its apologists stop short of calling it 'handsome'.

It does, nevertheless, have visually appealing features, for its neck and flanks are subtle in colour and pleasingly brindled, particularly in the southern race of this particular species (*Connochaetes taurinus*). The wildebeest found in northern Tanzania and in Kenya is darker and more uniform in colour, though it is compensated to some extent by having a characteristic white beard which its southern cousin lacks.

'Handsome is', of course, 'as handsome does' and, more important than looks, especially if you are a wildebeest, is the ability to survive in a fairly hostile environment, which is what the wildebeest, as a species, is extremely good at doing, as its numbers confirm. And in Ngorongoro survival skills, if you eat grass and are not an elephant, rhino or hippo, are well worth acquiring, for to a good many animals which share the 259 square kilometres (100 square miles) of the caldera floor you represent little more than the difference between a full belly and protein deficiency.

Opposite: Game drive takes the precipitous high road, hewn out of the cliff face, down to the Crater floor.

Above: Lion pride lolls on the shore of a waterhole inside the Crater, indifferent to the circle of game vehicles and watching tourists.

Opposite: Tourist's eye-view of the Crater floor from the lower reaches of the Seneto track.

One might imagine that a large antelope with potentially dangerous horns would use them in self-defence, as sable, roan, oryx, kudu and waterbuck are said to do, even against lions. But the wildebeest, when brought to bay, seems to 'give up the ghost' and allows itself to be downed and eaten with little more than a despairing or agonized groan.

Ironically a female wildebeest will vigorously defend her calf (with, it is reported, something like a thirty per cent success rate if all attacks are considered).

There is a theory that the greater the tendency of an animal to live in groups, the greater the tendency towards synchronized calving, which of course implies synchronized mating. It is certainly true in the case of the wildebeest of Ngorongoro where, as in the Serengeti, almost all calves are born in January or February.

The Ngorongoro wildebeest, incidentally, are to a large extent independent of the migratory herds of the Serengeti, though many of them do venture out of the Crater at times, just as some of the Serengeti animals sometimes move in.

Synchronized calving has obvious advantages among large numbers of animals in an open habitat, for even Ngorongoro's profusion of predators can only swallow so much over a short span of time. Calving in January or February also has advantages, for the grass at this time is green and nutritious. But there is little point in eating if you are soon to be eaten yourself, and the new-born wildebeest must learn, quite literally, to stand on its own feet. It does so with a precocity unknown in any other terrestrial mammal and, in an average time of seven minutes from the moment of birth, is able to run (albeit a little unsteadily) for its life. Times as short as four minutes have been recorded — pretty quick 'out of the blocks'

in life's uncertain race through the green and perilous pastures of Ngorongoro.

The wildebeest share these pastures with thousands of zebra, but they do not share the zebras' lifestyle. Grant's zebra (sometimes, apparently wrongly, referred to as Burchell's) is the only species found in Tanzania. It is known to live in family groups, consisting of a stallion, several mares and their foals, numbering in total anything up to fifteen animals. Each group is surprisingly stable in terms of consistent numbers of adults, and research in the Crater has indicated that families are held together by mutual consent of these adults rather than by the stallion's domination. Male wildebeest, on the other hand, set up seasonal territories — sometimes, during the migration, even on the move — and have a frantic time trying to control and mate with females who happen to pass through.

Competition for grazing among the many types of herbivore is said to be reduced by a natural 'grazing succession', with elephant, buffalo and zebra willing to move and feed among tall, fibrous grasses, followed by the more choosy feeders such as hartebeest which in turn are followed by the wildebeest and then the gazelle. Unlike the bovidae, which include antelope and buffalo, zebra have two sets of incisors and are therefore, it is argued, better able to nip off the stems of grass at a lower level. They are also believed to make more effective use of the sugar content of the grass than do the ruminants. Because zebra do not rechew their food, however, they still need to eat more, in ratio to their size, than antelopes and buffalo.

Hartebeest, though lacking the upper incisors of the zebra, are equipped with long narrow muzzles which allows greater selectivity and wildebeest, with their broader mouths, can 'mow' the grass almost as short as a well-kept lawn,

61

Above: The grounds and sparkling, turquoise pool of the Ngorongoro Sopa Lodge give unrivalled views of the Crater.

Right: The 100 luxury suites of the Ngorongoro Sopa Lodge nestle on the Crater rim amid luxuriant woodland.

Opposite: Herd of wildebeest, most numerous of Ngorongoro's mammal populations, stampede in alarm.

inadvertently leaving a safe yet sustaining habitat for the gazelle, which naturally prefer to stay in open, closely cropped areas.

Such theories will always be confounded, to some extent, by the perversity of the animals themselves, and elephant, buffalo and zebra can often be found feeding quite happily on short grass. Similarly the belief that certain larger herbivores create, however indirectly, suitable habitats for their smaller or more selective successors, is true only as far as it goes, for those animals which prefer open, short-grass areas can normally find them without too much help (other than that provided by the annual fires which have, for untold centuries, modified the African grasslands).

The zebra's role in the grazing succession might be important, but the animals are so aesthetically pleasing and so irresistibly photogenic that what they are actually doing and why they are doing it doesn't really seem to matter to many of us. Zebras are just good to look at. Mainly, of course, because of their striking markings, though these are as puzzling as they are dazzling. It used to be thought that the zebra's patterning was for camouflage purposes, though this received wisdom never seemed to allow for the glaring fact that there are few things in nature so dramatically conspicuous as a wild horse painted with black and white stripes. Fortunately for millions of human pedestrians, the designer of the 'zebra crossing' wasn't so naive.

The 'camouflage' notion was modified to fit the suggestion that at dawn and dusk (when lions were said to be very active) the zebra's stripes merged into a uniform grey. This is true, at least to human eyes, though it doesn't explain why zebras were not coloured grey in the first place. Nor does it take into

account the fact that the eyes of lions are exceptional at picking up the slightest of movements, even at dawn and dusk, and the stillest of zebras flicks its tail. One of several recent speculations is that the zebra's stripes are intended to confuse a predator as it rushes among a bolting family group. Who knows? Could it just be possible that whoever designed the zebra had shares in Kodak — or some other film company?

The stripes are excellent focusing aids for a cameraman but they are also an aid to identification. Every zebra has its individual arrangement of stripes, though you could easily go cross-eyed trying to convince yourself. To what extent zebras themselves depend upon these patterns for mutual recognition is unclear, though it is known that mixed herds of zebra and wildebeest will separate when panicked by predators, whereas mixed herds of Grevy's and Common zebras will remain together, despite being disparate species. What is perhaps more interesting is that zebra society, unusually in a vulnerable prey species, is a relatively caring one. Fit and healthy individuals, contrary to the belief that such creatures 'look after number one' while their less fortunate companions are ruthlessly isolated and killed, have been known to show concern for old or sick family members, and even provide actual assistance.

Another striped animal in Ngorongoro (though the stripes are much less obvious) is the eland, largest of the antelope, weighing — at about 900 kilos (1,980lbs) — considerably more than ten times the weight of an average man. They are often described as 'cow-like', though the resemblance is superficial and, despite their size, are able to leap two metres (six-and-a-half feet) into the air with apparent ease, and keep up a running trot for many kilometres.

Opposite: Alert zebra keep watchful eye for passing predators.

Below: Zebra cool off in the alkaline waters of Lake Makat, also known as Magadi.

Hunters and wildlife photographers will bear witness to their nervousness when approached for, even in well patrolled game sanctuaries, they will often flee long before a reasonable photograph can be taken. The much used (and practically meaningless) phrase 'The Real Africa' means different things to different people but to see a herd of eland trotting high-headed through the middle distance of a wild and seemingly endless African landscape must merit a place in the myth.

You are hardly likely to see such a sight in the Crater, where the eland are untypically calm, but the rare chance to get close to a creature which has been called 'the apotheosis of antelope evolution' is not such a bad consolation. The onlooker will usually be able to contrast its great size with that of a nearby gazelle, which make up in numbers and slender grace for what they lack in bulk, and which are seen almost everywhere on the Crater floor.

The word 'gazelle' is derived from Arabic and the true antelopes, all small to medium-sized and delicate in build, are mostly gazelle. Two species are found in Ngorongoro, named after the nineteenth-century British explorers Thomson and Grant. 'Tommies', as the popular diminutive implies, inspire affection in all but the most pedestrian of observers. They weigh only twenty-five kilos (55lbs) or so (about one-third the weight of the Grant's) but their small bodies are full of vitality and their switching tails are never still.

They are also visually attractive. The contrast between their glistening, sandy-coloured coats and pure white bellies is heavily accentuated by the broad, slanting black band across the lower flanks, reminiscent of the eye-catching flashes one sees on so much 'designer' sportswear. The Grant's gazelle, as well as being noticeably bigger, is paler in tone, its lateral

68

stripe much less distinct and the white of its buttock region extending a little way above the tail (distinguishing it from the 'Tommy' when size is difficult to assess).

Gazelle are adapted to dry conditions but another of Ngorongoro's antelope, the grey, shaggy but stately water-buck, is as dependent upon water as its name suggests. It can often be seen along the fringes of the Lerai Forest, but it is one of the few species at Ngorongoro which seems equally at home on the forested rim or in the Crater itself. Males defend territories quite vigorously against other mature males, yet access to water is apparently never denied, even to a potentially threatening intruder. 'Chivalry', at least among the waterbuck, is not yet dead. The Maasai name for the waterbuck is 'the one with the white bottom', for obvious reasons — the race of waterbuck found in Ngorongoro, the Defassa, has a white rump (opposed to the Common, the rump of which bears a white circle).

The Bohor reedbuck, another animal which is never found too far from water, is less easily observed, for it survives by keeping, often literally, a low profile, lying up among reeds or long grass in places such as the Munge Swamp. At the approach of a large predator a reedbuck will sometimes lie flat with neck outstretched, leaping up only at the last moment, perhaps with a loud whistle of alarm. In flight they can be recognized by their 'rocking-horse' gait. Like the waterbuck, males are territorial, and are said to be pugnacious in captivity.

An antelope notable for its absence from the caldera is the impala, though they are found in the Conservation Area itself and are common in parts of the adjacent Serengeti and nearby Manyara. They are among the most elegant of animals and to

*Above: Impala in flight.
These beautiful antelope do
not inhabit the Crater but
graze in large numbers in the
Ngorongoro Conservation
Unit.*

*Right: Shy Bohor reedbuck,
one of two reedbuck species
found in the Crater.*

*Opposite: Beautifully
proportioned, spiral horns of
a Defassa waterbuck found in
abundance around the
seasonal lakes, waterholes
and swamps of the Crater and
its forests.*

see them leaping, their red-brown coats gleaming in the sun and the rams with their gracefully shaped horns thrown back, is one of natural Africa's aesthetic experiences — a ballet of the wild.

Other absentee herbivores from the Crater are the giraffe and wart hog (though the Maasai say that these have been seen in the Crater in the past) and elephants other than bulls. Giraffe are often seen on the western rim as one drives down to the plains, for like the impala they prefer acacia woodlands to open grassland, but wart hogs, in common with the two other pigs found in the Conservation Area, the nocturnal bush pig and the giant forest hog, are not seen frequently — if at all — by visitors.

Elephant can also be elusive in Ngorongoro, despite their size. They too seem to prefer wooded habitats if these are available, which might explain the absence of cows and calves from the Crater. Bulls tend to be more adventurous (or less circumspect) and move in and out of the caldera as the mood takes them, though even they tend to seek food in the shady security of the Lerai or among the long grasses and reeds which fringe the Munge Swamp. There was, at least in the early 'eighties and despite the heavy poaching of elephants at that time, a particularly fine bull living in the Lerai area, carrying heavy ivory for those perilous times.

Hippo are not numerous in the Crater either, for obvious reasons, but they can be seen at the so-called Hippo Pool at the fringes of the Gorgor Swamp, just to the east of the Lerai. Many people, standing on the banks of the pool and looking down on these amusingly dumpy creatures, which seem to have been created to have their images carved from soapstone by African craftsmen, must wonder how such corpulent and

apparently indolent mammals ever came to find themselves at the bottom of an extinct volcano in the Tanzanian highlands.

The answer is simple — they walked there. The 'Hippo Pool', as the Pied crow flies, is only thirty kilometres (eighteen miles) from Lake Eyasi and forty (twenty-five miles) from Lake Manyara, and hippos are surprisingly mobile, often travelling many kilometres overnight, when they leave the water to graze. They are not as docile, either, as their 'cuddly' roundedness might suggest — even lions treat them with respect and hippos cause a good many deaths and injuries to fishermen and villagers along some of Africa's waterways. When unmolested and in the water, however, they present no danger as long as you don't pose a threat by approaching too closely on foot.

Another potentially dangerous but normally docile herbivore found in Ngorongoro (but again not always plentiful in the Crater) is the buffalo. Like the other members of the 'Big Five', the buffalo gained its reputation in the heyday of the 'White Hunter', and with good reason. A wounded or threatened buffalo is basically 600-800 kilos (1,320-1,760lbs) of malicious muscle and bone with a massive set of cargo hooks at the business end. Even in areas where they are no longer persecuted, the buffalo commands huge respect among rangers, game scouts and other 'old Africa hands' who might find themselves on foot in the bush.

In 1964 an enraged buffalo in the Ngorongoro area impaled a Maasai warrior on his own spear — the classic 'Man Bites Dog' story on an African scale. The Maasai, walking with a friend, had been charged by the buffalo and hurled his spear at the animal. The opposing forces of spear and buffalo resulted in the spear being lodged in the animal's forehead, and the

Above: Hippo wallow in the waters of Ngorongoro Crater's hippo pool. Nocturnal grazers, these mammoths of East Africa's waterways migrate large distances between lakes and rivers.

Opposite: Maasai giraffe abound in the savannah bushlands of the Ngorongoro Conservation Unit and sometimes graze the Crater floor.

buffalo continued its charge with the six-foot weapon projecting from its head, spearing the Maasai through the chest with the pointed haft. The wounded man's friend finished off the buffalo and the injured man, one lung punctured, was taken to Arusha hospital, where he eventually recovered.

Generally, however, buffalo are peaceful animals, though a large breeding herd, several hundred strong, can give a newcomer to the bush something to worry about when its members 'threaten' to crowd the visitor's vehicle. The air of menace is more often due to myopia — buffalo are short-sighted and will sometimes approach a vehicle to determine its motives. A clap of the hands will usually stampede the largest herd, though the best response is to sit still and enjoy the sight of one of Africa's legendary 'Big Five' at close quarters.

All Ngorongoro's herbivores are interesting in their way. 'When you've seen one zebra you've seen them all' is not the catchphrase of the genuinely interested observer, however inexperienced, and antelopes are 'boring' only to those who have little curiosity, or who have forgotten how to look at life through the eyes of a child. But all visitors to Ngorongoro want to see one herbivore more than any other, for it isn't every day that one can see and photograph a prehistoric monster.

The rhino certainly looks as if it should be extinct — and of course, with the help of a small percentage of unscrupulous and highly motivated men, it almost is. Everyone knows who is to blame — 'the foreigners'. 'They' are usually African, Indian, Arab, Chinese or seedy entrepreneurs from Hong Kong. And if you look closely at the highly organized

poaching networks which until recently were working so efficiently to rid the Earth of the rhino, you will indeed see that individuals and gangs from these racial groups were directly or indirectly responsible. But it doesn't do for Westerners to get too self-righteous — much of the carved ivory taken from elephants finished up in the West and John Alexander Hunter, the British safari guide and hunter who was mentioned earlier, shot 996 rhino between 29 August 1944 and 31 October 1946, within sixty miles of Nairobi, at the request of the colonial government.

He was, of course, a man of his time, well-respected and engaged in business which he, and the government officials who employed him, felt to be necessary and worthwhile — and rhinos were obviously not on the endangered list in those days. But the desperately poor African at the bottom of the putrid poaching pyramid might fail to appreciate such fine distinctions. Fortunately more enlightened people, from all parts of the world, together with the brave front-line support of the best of Africa's wardens and rangers, have slowed the slaughter almost to a stop — at least in most places, and certainly in the Crater.

It will take years for rhino populations to recover. Rhino have a gestation period of seventeen to eighteen months and only breed every three years or so, but when a male and a receptive female get together they make the most of it — coition can last for thirty or forty minutes or more, during which the male might ejaculate several times. This tenacity of purpose resulted, over the centuries and until the middle of this one, in a pretty healthy rhino population, not least in Ngorongoro.

Baumann talked of ' . . . a pleasant acacia forest by a lake',

Above: Cape buffalo, most ferocious of Africa's Big Five when aroused are rarely aggressive in the peaceful environment of the Crater.

Opposite: Rare survivor of Ngorongoro's once-abundant rhino population.

near which 'the plain was again populated by numerous rhinos, amongst which there were magnificent snow-white specimens'. More than seventy years later the intrepid biologist John Goddard (who did a lot of his research on foot and unarmed) could still find one hundred and ten rhinos in the Crater and seventy more at Olduvai Gorge. As late as 1970 there were twenty-three rhino in the Lerai Forest alone — nineteen to the square mile (more than seven per square kilometre).

Rhino, despite their bulk — a full-grown one weighs in at 700-1600 kilos (1,540-3,520lbs), or half an elephant — are deceptively nimble on their feet. They can stop in full charge and spin around to face the opposite direction, all within a few seconds. Their reputation for unpredictability is well justified, though they are not as aggressive as is sometimes made out. Like most big game they will normally avoid confrontation with Man, and their so-called 'charges', when they take place at all, are usually exploratory rushes to frighten away intruders or to determine the source of a potential threat (the rhino's eyesight is very poor but movement and noise on the part of an intruder would be quickly registered).

It was still possible in the late 'seventies, assuming you were lucky and accompanied by a good guide, to see twelve or more rhino on the Crater floor in a single day. Sometimes, in places such as the splendidly silvery grasslands by Layanai, beyond Kitate Hill, a small group of them might be encountered, not quite snow-white like Baumann's, but greyish-white for the same reasons (having wallowed in alkaline mud). Visitors would have to be lucky and persistent to see such groups and numbers today, though the situation is gradually improving.

Following pages: Two-way traffic — brought to the brink of extinction by poaching, the numbers of black rhino within the Crater and the Conservation Unit are now increasing.

Most people, however, should see at least one, and one rhino is well worth seeing. You might even find a cow with calf, which is always a reassuring thrill and, if you follow the advice of an experienced guide, you will be able to approach quite closely without danger. Occasionally an individual rhino in the Crater will give visitors more excitement than they bargained for, but actual damage to vehicles is rare and minimal, and the guides (who should never be tempted to provoke animals) know what they are doing.

5. Golden Lions

After rhinos the Crater's biggest attraction, as in so many other places, is the lion. All three of the big African cats are found in Ngorongoro, though you will need luck, as mentioned earlier, to see leopards, and even cheetahs (*Acinonyx jubatus*) — the cats without fully retractible claws. Regularly seen on the nearby Serengeti plains, they can be hard to find in the Crater, which makes sighting them all the more rewarding.

When cheetahs are around, being more diurnal than most cats, they are most likely to be visible standing or sitting on prominent features of the terrain, such as rocks or termite mounds, from which advantage points they can look around for likely prey. This includes Grant's and Thomson's gazelles, hares, bustards and guinea fowl.

Some people regard them as the most beautiful of all the cats. With their streamlined build and their golden coats scattered with black spots (singly and not in groups of five like the leopard) and their very distinctive black facial stripes running from side of eye to side of mouth, they are certainly pleasing to look upon. But it is their reputation as the world's fastest mammal which catches the imagination. They are the 'greyhounds of the Felidae', the cat family which also includes the lion, leopard, caracal, serval and African wildcat, all of which make Eastern Africa their home.

The cheetah is indeed capable of exceptional speed, though observers are sometimes surprised and perhaps disappointed to find that many attempts to bring down prey are carried out at a pace which is impressive rather than astonishing, and many chases are unsuccessful. To effect the kill, the cheetah needs to knock its victim's hind feet from under it with its forepaw, then strangle it by seizing its throat, somehow

finding the breath to perform this major final assault at the end of a lung-bursting chase.

After the kill, if there is a family of young, or pride amongst which it must be shared, the cheetah's eating behaviour, compared with some of the other carnivores, is little short of delicate. Ever on the alert against larger, thieving predators, the pride eats in unquarrelsome relays (leaving those who are not eating to guard) until all are fed, displaying control and fastidious 'table manners' rarely witnessed in the wild.

Kill they obviously must to survive (often Thomson's gazelle where these are plentiful), but being basically gentle and timid animals, they often lose their prize to lions and even hyenas or vultures.

Lions will sometimes drive cheetahs from their pride's home range and, not being good climbers (though they climb more often than is sometimes thought), cheetahs have to be constantly wary. They must also avoid injury. This is not easy for a creature which often sprints across hard-baked earth littered with stones, thorns or burrows. Even a septic foot might mean a lingering death.

It has been said that continent-wide, their range is shrinking, and as a result they are a diminishing species. They are already extinct in northern and southern Africa.

Leopards and cheetahs might be hard to come by in the Crater, but lions are almost guaranteed. Yet despite their relative abundance the sighting of a lion, no matter how many have been seen previously, rarely loses its thrill. That moment, usually early in the morning, when a patch of grass or a small termite mound or some other indistinct and tawny-grey part of the landscape resolves itself into a lion, is endlessly magical. For bound up in that powerful and familiar profile is all that

Right: Black-maned lion, victor in many battles for supremacy, rests on the Crater floor through the midday heat — photographic trophy for delighted tourists.

other more mysterious power, derived from centuries of myth and fear and ancient symbolism, which gives the lion its unceasing allure.

You would have to try hard to miss them on the caldera floor, though a lion can lie hidden in the flimsiest of cover, especially when lying on its side, for lions are amazingly slim in section. Even when lying in the open they are not always easy to distinguish, but in the Crater they are never far away. They might, however, seem deceptively inactive once they are found, for by the time most visitors are successfully ferried down the Seneto track, the morning's activity is virtually over for most lions, and they will be flopped as placidly as golden labradors in the strengthening sun.

The Ngorongoro lions (there are about 100 in the Crater) do seem to have a more golden coat than the greyer lions seen in the south, but any resemblance to labradors ends with their colour, their smooth sleek lines (when relaxed) and their relatively big paws. They are cats and they are killers, and what you see as they sprawl in the sun is not placidity, but ferocity on standby.

Lions are opportunists and will hunt at any time, but the experienced ones have an intuitive ability to weigh probable gain, in terms of food, against probable loss in terms of energy. Young animals or cubs might set off on some futile stalk, but the 'old hands' will stay put if the odds of making a kill seem too unfavourable. After nine or ten in the morning, especially if the sun is hot, you are unlikely to see lions hunt, though they sometimes do, and the least promising of situations can change within minutes into a fascinating drama.

Like all cats lions have good night vision yet, interestingly, their eyes (and the eyes of all the *Panthera* genus) have round

pupils, in contrast with the elliptical pupils of the small cats, including the domestic. Most hunting probably takes place at night and in the cool of the early morning, when the advantage lies more with the lions and when they tend to be more alert and restless. When they do hunt they are so different from their resting stereotype as to seem almost another species. A stalking lion is the embodiment of feline intent — economy of movement combined with concentrated purpose, and an ability, both innate and learned, to take maximum advantage of available cover (though not, surprisingly, of wind direction).

They are said to be inefficient, in the sense that roughly seven out of ten attempts to kill are abortive, a ratio which might even be too charitable to the lion. But if you could work out the average amount of energy expended by a lion in order to keep itself in food, you would find that they get by quite nicely — after all, they are hardly in danger of starving themselves into extinction. If being inefficient hunters allows them to spend twenty to twenty-one hours a day at rest (or copulating) then what lion needs the Protestant work-ethic?

Lions are unusual among the cats for being social, though some authorities believe that this aspect of their lives developed comparatively recently and that they haven't fully adjusted to it. They have certainly learned to co-operate when hunting, and also to employ forward-thinking strategies. Convincing evidence of this has been recorded on several occasions, and there is an excellent piece of film showing lions in the Crater setting up a fairly elaborate ambush in the Mundusi Swamp.

Lions might stand accused of being inefficient hunters but they excel in at least one collaborative act — the sexual one.

Above: The largest of Africa's three big cats, the lion is inherently lazy. But deceptively so for it can clear a barrier four metres (thirteen feet) high or a chasm twelve metres (thirty feet) wide at one leap.

Opposite: Lioness with cubs. Significantly, Ngorongoro's lion families are under threat through inbreeding.

The lions in Ngorongoro are always, it appears, 'at it'. Perhaps this is an illusion — it is easier to be a voyeur in an enclosed open space than in a habitat with more cover. Or perhaps there is 'something in the air' in the Crater. Or maybe there is, in that bowl of plenty, little else for them to do. Whatever the case, the number of leonine liaisons in Ngorongoro can be quite staggering — especially, one might think, if you happen to be a male lion.

Lionesses, like all female cats, need the stimulation of repeated copulation in order to ovulate. When in oestrus they behave in a 'precocious' manner which might earn them, were they young and human and surrounded by moralistic maiden aunts, a 'shameless hussy' reputation. Males subjected to such unambiguous attentions have been known to be put off rather than turned on, and, when we learn what is required of them, one is tempted to say 'No wonder!'.

One particular lion was seen to mate 157 times in fifty-five hours, eighty-six of these during the course of the first day (sharing himself with two females). During the second twenty-four-hour period he mated a further sixty-two times and in the remaining seven hours nine times more. The drastic rate of decline is hardly surprising and neither is the fact that male lions sometimes work in relays, for a lioness might be in oestrus for three to five days or even as long as a fortnight. Any extra male waiting to go 'on shift' does so without apparent 'jealousy' — presumably contented in the knowledge that his turn is bound to come.

Because of the relatively isolated nature of the Crater, the behaviour and even the bodies of its lions are changing. When you see mating lions there, you are often witnessing incest.

Such behaviour, and many other fascinating aspects of lion

society, can be watched at close hand by a sensitive observer, thanks to the indifference with which lions generally treat vehicles. Whether the behaviour under scrutiny is mating, feeding, stalking or even killing, the tactful driver can place himself and any passengers right alongside leonine action and interaction. An experienced observer, however, will know when to move in and when to stay back, and will avoid interfering in a hunt or disturbing a delicate situation or nervous individual.

If a car is small, the close proximity of large predators may be worrying, but there is little danger, providing the occupants behave sensibly. The insights gained are often so intimate that one almost feels part of the pride, and part of an absorbing drama; a soap opera of the wild. Sometimes these shows of warm fellowship become rather too intimate, for lions are tactile creatures which love to rub heads and flanks when greeting pridemates, and a nearby car might occasionally be included in the rituals.

Life at the top of the food chain, even in Ngorongoro, isn't always as agreeable as it might seem. Lions are quite commonly injured when hunting or during feeding or territorial squabbles (in which extended claws can be the order of the day), and even kings are mortal — lions have lived for thirty years in captivity but it seems unlikely that a male lion in the wild would survive much more than twelve to fifteen. In Ngorongoro, which contains the largest concentration of carnivores in the world, lions tend to live shorter lives than the general average — due, perhaps, to greater stress.

Old males, especially, often bear terrible traces of life's misfortunes. You might see lions in the Crater with only one good eye, or 'cauliflower' ears, or faces scarified, over the

94

Opposite: Lioness with kill. On average, a lion or lioness account for nineteen head of game a year at a weight of about 115 kilos (250lbs) for each kill.

Above: Lions mate with extraordinary frequency — often more than 200 times a day. The act is brief — rarely lasting more than thirty seconds.

Opposite: Pride rests up alongside an Ngorongoro Crater waterhole. Lion rarely hunt during the heat of day, tending to stalk either in the early morning or late afternoon.

years, by a variety of raking claws. Missing tail tips, torn ears, broken and worn teeth and badly injured legs or feet are not unusual. Like many animals lions often recover from the most awful looking wounds and disabilities, but persisting or severe injuries can put a lion out of action or contention, and that means, at worst, a drawn out death from starvation.

Death comes in many forms, for lions as for humans, but for a lion to die of hunger in the Crater must be the cruellest of ironies, for the estimated biomass of prey species is an astounding 26,308 kilos (58,000lbs) per two-and-a-half square kilometres or per square mile. As there are perhaps fifty to seventy lions on the floor of the Crater at any one time, this works out at something like 15,422 kilos (34,000lbs) of potential food for each one, a figure which seems less dramatic when we read that there are also 370 spotted hyenas in the same area, and that the spotted hyena in Ngorongoro is primarily a killer rather than a scavenger, and therefore a serious competitor of the lion.

Yet lions often starve to death, as cubs. Perhaps as many as half of them die before the age of two. Few wild lions make it into old age, especially the males, many of which die violently in fights with other males or, when they wander outside the parks and reserves, at the hands of Man. Those lions which survive such dangers, and the various accidents or diseases which threaten all living creatures, might enjoy their prime but they have little to look forward to when feebleness finally overtakes them.

There can be few more moving and melancholy sights in the wild than to witness the end of an animal so long acknowledged, in myth and folklore and maybe in our collective subconsciousness, as 'king'. Death and dying con-

front every traveller in the bush, carcasses corrupt the thick air with the stomach-turning stench of their own decomposition, and bones and skulls, especially in the dry season, catch the eye in an environment prejudiced against whiteness. But there is an atavistic abhorrence in beholding the dying of a lion.

Hyenas, with less imposing anthropomorphic associations, haven't had a good press in the past, but in these more enlightened times are much better understood, and if to know them is not exactly to love them, no one can deny that they are interesting animals, with a functional perfection which in itself is a kind of beauty. The Crater is one of the best places to appreciate this consummate product of evolution, for hyenas are not only numerous there but much more diurnal in habit than in most other places.

Above: Young adult cheetah relax in the shade.

Above: Cheetah are the most specialised of the killer cats and the most vulnerable. Timid and gentle, their kills are often snatched away by lion or hyena — while leopard stalk young cheetah cubs.

6. The Predator — Spotted Hyena

The Spotted hyena (the only one found in Ngorongoro except for rare sightings of the Striped) is the largest, commonest, most widespread and most aggressive of the three African species, and the most important predator in the Crater in terms of its impact upon prey species.

Research (much of it carried out in the Crater) has shown that spotted hyenas, despite their reputation as 'cringing' and 'cowardly' scavengers and their continuing association with witchcraft among certain African tribes are bold and effective killers, especially by night. They will attack and devour a lion which is unable to defend itself, have been known to attack people sleeping in the open, and are said to kill, each year, about one-quarter of the wildebeest calves born in the Crater.

Their social structure and behaviour within the Crater is perhaps modified by the nature of the caldera itself, with its abundance of prey and its high retaining walls. Certainly the number of hyena found there suggests an optimum population density and a perfect habitat (apparently the density of hyenas in Ngorongoro is fourteen times as great as that in the nearby Serengeti). These hyenas, unlike many outside the Crater, are often seen in large groups, and studies suggest that there are about eight clans on the caldera floor, each containing between ten and 100 members including males, females and cubs.

Although there is some fluidity of movement between these clans, the borders of their territories are generally jealously guarded; interlopers being chased away and sometimes attacked. The Spotted hyena is well equipped for chasing and attacking — all its power seems concentrated in the relatively massive forequarters, with its sturdy forelegs and lungs

providing stamina and the shorter, lighter hind legs helping to give thrust and acceleration.

Its jaws are fearsome. The cutting edges of their upper and lower carnassial teeth come together with such shearing leverage that they can crack the leg-bone of a hippopotamus. It is reported that hyenas can chew and digest a galvanized iron bucket (though why they should choose to do so remains an intriguing mystery). What they undoubtedly do, at least in Ngorongoro, where they are almost exclusively hunters rather than scavengers, is to bring down prey as large as full-grown wildebeest and zebra and, less often, eland and buffalo.

Adult wildebeest and zebra are, it seems, hunted only at night, and by different methods. Only one to three hyenas are usually involved in the hunting of wildebeest and, having selected a victim, give chase and bring the animal to a standstill by snapping at its legs and loins. A single hyena can bring to a stop and disembowel a full-grown wildebeest, with only token resistance from the unfortunate victim.

Adult zebras are hunted at night also, but by much larger packs, perhaps because zebra stallions show much more spirit than wildebeest and will defend the mares and foals. A zebra hunt is a deliberate enterprise preceded by elaborate rituals. Once a chase is under way, individual hyenas will try to outflank the stallion to attack a more vulnerable member of the family group. Once such an animal is isolated and surrounded by hyenas the stallion will no longer try to help, and the victim will succumb resignedly to disembowelment, though death comes more quickly, because of the greater numbers of predators. Disposal also comes quickly — a pack of hyenas was once seen to devour a complete adult zebra within fifteen minutes.

Above: Hyena circles buffalo skeleton as a flock of vultures picks it clean.

Opposite: Hyena cubs stay close to den in long grass. Studies show the hyena is the most efficient of all Ngorongoro predators, accounting for more kills than any other species.

Hyenas hunt and kill a variety of other animals (ninety-three per cent of carcasses examined in the Crater were those of animals killed by hyenas) but if they live by the sword they also die by it. Their life expectancy in the Crater is only, at best, about twelve or thirteen years, as opposed to about twenty-five in captivity, and when their hour comes it comes without compassion. Out of twenty-four hyenas found dead in Ngorongoro, thirteen had been killed by lions, four by other hyenas, two by humans and five had died from starvation or disease.

Death at least is decisive. Life, especially for a male hyena, must be more confusing. For a start, female hyenas, unusually among mammals, are bigger and dominant and are, on the whole, more high-ranking. It is not merely size which determines this superiority — if we accept the interpretations of the scientists — but personality and behaviour. Hans Kruuk, whose research in Ngorongoro provided so many surprises about the amazing life of the hyena, speculated that the dominance of the female is evolution's answer to that other aspect of the hyena's character, it's somewhat disagreeable tendency to eat other hyenas (mainly, of course, the cubs, which the larger and more imposing females can protect).

As if all this weren't enough, the male hyena cannot even rely on his masculinity to give him sexual status, for female equality among hyenas has been taken, by nature, extremely seriously, so much so that the hyena has often been thought of as hermaphrodite. The females' genitalia exactly resembles that of the males in shape and size, even when erect. All sorts of speculations have been made about the positions adopted by mating hyenas in order to reconcile the imagined

bewilderment of the male when faced with a demanding partner who looks just like himself, but bigger.

The sheer numbers of hyenas, and the fluffy black cubs which are sometimes seen outside their dens in Ngorongoro, are living proof of the male hyena's ability to fulfil his sexual role, which he accomplishes in the dog-like position one might expect. More unexpectedly he achieves penetration by inserting his penis into the clitoris of the female which, during copulation, is not erect and which encompasses the urogenital tract. No one can say that hyenas are boring.

If in the distance, and without the aid of binoculars to clarify its identity, you see a medium-largish, somewhat untidy-looking creature lolloping across the Crater floor with what appears to be a black sock hanging from its mouth, out of kindness resist the temptation to give chase to gain closer inspection. It will more than probably be a desperate hyena, from one of the hyena clans which inhabit the Crater, rushing one of its young away to a place it believes to be safer than the one from which circumstances have driven it. It may run distractedly for great distances further than it needs and into hostile territory if relentlessly pursued by curious spectators in the comfort of a four-wheel drive vehicle or a minibus. But it will not drop its burden.

Unlike the cheetah, the hyena is not built for high speeds and — without any intention of making this 'Beastly to Hyenas Year' by commenting adversely on its design, for which it was not responsible — its gait is anything but dignified.

However, its effort to protect its young is commendable by any standards, and the cub will lie relaxed and passive between those fearsome jaws until the parent, with its

Opposite: Wart hog are not endemic in Ngorongoro Crater but flourish in abundance throughout the rest of the Conservation Unit.

Above: Vultures and marabou stork pick the bones of a buffalo kill clean.

Opposite: Golden jackal with small prey.

'animated black sock' passenger, has fled the real or imagined danger zone.

Unlike lions, hyenas are rarely seen mating and in some areas rarely seen at all by day. In Ngorongoro they are also predominantly nocturnal but, perhaps because of the open country, the climate and their population densities, are very much in evidence. By night, should you be in your tent on the Crater floor or sitting in silence outside your lodge, you will almost certainly hear their haunting and sometimes disturbing calls, familiar to all who camp in the African bush. This well-known 'Whoo-eee-whoo-oop!' is one of the most evocative sounds of the African night, almost as nostalgic as the imploring call of the lion, with its repetitive, moaning cadence and the plaintive, insistent, far-carrying call of the African fish eagle.

The hyena's whooping call is heard much more often than the hysterical giggling and chuckling which gave rise to the nickname 'laughing hyena'. This demoniacal din is inspired by high excitement and sometimes fear, during disputes between clans or in the frenzy surrounding a kill. At such times the collective cacophony sounds fit to raise the dead, more reminiscent of a coven of deranged witches than a gathering of wild animals.

But even this sepulchral din is transcended in chilling intensity by the call of another nocturnal creature found in Ngorongoro. Campers at the Fig Tree campsite in the Crater, a place dominated by the superb fig tree which gives the spot its name, might find themselves awakened at about that time in the night when moral courage, according to Napoleon Bonaparte, is at its least prepared. The immediate cause of their awakening will have been a most unearthly scream, the

108

climax to a nightmarish sequence of noises which begin with a low groaning, rising to a ratchet-like noise, like that of certain fishing reels being turned very slowly under great resistance.

This noise increases ominously in volume and tempo, to be suddenly terminated by the drawn-out scream, followed by an equally ominous silence, before the groaning starts up all over again. It can be most unnerving, unless you know that it emerges from the vocal chords of a small and harmless arboreal creature, the Tree hyrax — a little like a rabbit without the long ears. The climactic scream can be heard up to three kilometres away. The effects of this upon a camper sleeping soundly under the hyraxes' tree can be imagined.

Following pages: Elephant take water and feed on the grasses of one of the Crater's permanent swamps. Fed by Ngorongoro's freshwater streams, the soda lake, hippo pool and swamps provide the essential permanent pastures that sustain the Crater's wildlife populations. Without them, the resident herbivores would join the mass migrations of the Serengeti in search of pasture.

7. Splendours of the Crater

All this talk of death and nightmares seems a long way from the beauty of Ngorongoro, and yet death with its piquancy of excitement and fear, are integral to the Crater's nature and attraction. Ngorongoro is not a zoo or a 'safari park'. It is the real thing. Animals kill and are killed, often violently, and the human history of the area has not always been a peaceful one. The landscape itself is violence petrified. The apparent tranquillity one sees from the lodges on the Crater rim, and even to a large extent from the caldera floor, is in fact an equilibrium of unresolved tensions and conflicts, though this too has an intricate primitive beauty.

Even among the birds and insects, the flowers and grasses and trees, which so often to us are symbols of peace and beauty, there exists an endless competition — for space or food or sexual opportunity or some other urgent need. It is hardly possible to touch upon this multitude of creatures and plants in a book as short as this; the bird species alone, within a 160-kilometre (100 mile) radius of the Crater, number more than 500, from the tiny sunbirds to the Kori bustards, which can stand three feet tall, with long, powerful legs and with lax-feathered necks, beautifully vermiculated black and grey.

The Kori bustard looks big at any time, but in display the male seems even bigger, his neck inflated and his tail cocked upside down against his back. How even a female bustard can find this grotesque posture attractive is difficult to imagine, though there is nothing, I suppose, more ludicrous than human males when passion overtakes us.

When passion overtakes the biggest of all birds, the ostrich, we are in the superleague of feather-ruffling fornication. The ostrich, perfectly at home on the open swards of the Crater floor, is familar to everyone, though the sexes look slightly

different, the male being black and white whereas the female's wings and back are a brownish grey. The ostrich's wings are useless in themselves but during the courtship display they become elegant accessories in a remarkable dance-like ritual, during which the female is furiously chased by the male, both birds strutting and weaving in a jerky flurry of legs and feathers.

The male's neck becomes an inflamed red when in mating condition, though as the ostrich is the only bird equipped with a proper penis, and as this penis, when tumescent, is in proportion to the considerable size of the bird, any colour-coding of the neck (if such it is) would seem to be superfluous. The condition and intentions of the male could scarcely be in doubt. The apparently harassed female (she is, in fact, almost certainly 'leading him on', as female ostriches initiate events with a vibrant quivering of wings) eventually crouches in a submissive, trembling mass of plumage and pulsating wings, allowing the male to mount. After a minute or so of swaying from side to side he steps back, his long, grooved penis falling flaccid between his thighs.

Another outlandish bird — or rather many hundreds of them — can be easily found in the Crater, along the shorelines of Lake Makat (Magadi), though unlike the ostrich it doesn't breed in Ngorongoro. In fact, as late as 1951, Mackworth-Praed and Grant, authors of what was then the standard handbook of East African birds, wrote of the Lesser flamingo; 'There is no bird of its size and numbers in accessible parts of the world about which so little is known'.

Its breeding habits were certainly obscure until the late, intrepid Leslie Brown, one of East Africa's foremost authorities on birds, discovered nesting colonies on the mud-flats of Lake

113

Above: Hen ostrich with brood in tow on the Crater floor.

Left: Ostrich cock turns red with passion as it goes into mating mode.

Opposite: Kori bustard blows up ruff of neck feathers during mating display.

Natron, just outside the Conservation Area to the north-east. Leslie stripped the soles off his feet and almost died of dehydration while crossing the caustic soda to confirm his discovery. Years later he wrote, 'No bird or animal that I have ever studied has forced me to such extremes of effort and suffering. And none has ever given me such a reward of beauty and excitement'.

Exciting flamingos might be and, at least when considered collectively, quite beautiful. It is astonishing that birds so ungainly and ugly in the singular should, en masse and at a reasonable distance, look so entrancing. It is, of course, their soft and beautiful shades of pink and red, multiplied by hundreds or thousands and mirrored in the still waters which they frequent, which so delight us.

What is more surprising, when you see them in the wild, is their collective noise, for their deep murmurations, honks and grunts are as unlikely as the birds themselves. You will often see the two East African species, the Greater and the Lesser, in the same company in the Crater, though the former is a bottom feeder in slightly deeper water, its angled bill inverted and pointing backwards as it strains larvae from the mud. The Lesser merely skims the water of the inshore shallows, its diet consisting of microscopic blue-green algae and diatoms. Apart from these dissimilarities in habit and the noticeable size difference implicit in their names, the Greater is paler, with a pink, black-tipped bill, while the plumage of the Lesser is a deeper and brighter pink and its bill carmine red.

Makat does not attract the spectacular numbers of flamingos which can sometimes be seen in the Rift Valley lakes such as Nakuru, though the crater lake in Empakaai, some thirty kilometres (eighteen miles) to the north-east of Ngorongoro

Crater, can be, at certain times, quite rewarding, and is worth the visit in any case. But the flamingos at Makat are not to be overlooked.

In flight, like so many of the larger storks, herons and pelicans, the gawky-looking flamingo is transformed into a bird of easy, soaring grace. A flock of flamingos in the air is a sight to remember, and a pink foam of flamingos along a lakeshore difficult to forget. But Ngorongoro is rich in memorable bird species — not all of which are as eye-catching as the ostrich or as gaudy as the flamingo. There are glamourous species among the smaller birds, such as the Rosy-breasted longclaw, which adorns the short grass plains like some occasional, exotic flower, or that exquisite little waxbill the Purple Grenadier, or the brilliant sunbirds, but there is an understated beauty too in the delicate lines and plumage of the larks and pipits, and in the migrant waders with their unpretentious northern pallor, or in the subtle spotting and barring of the game birds, such as the guinea-fowl and spurfowl.

Even some mammals, such as the wild dog, occasional visitor to the Crater, have had to be overlooked. And what of the splendid butterflies and other insects? And the plants — for we musn't forget that much of Ngorongoro's beauty is founded on grass — near-sacred to the Maasai, those natural 'Go Green' environmentalists, and essential, directly or otherwise, to all the creatures in this quite remarkable region. If only there were space and time to take a longer and more probing look at Ngorongoro, and see it, as the poet William Blake would have us see the world, 'in a grain of sand' (or in this case lava), to talk of birds and butterflies and bats, and to consider the lilies of the field, and how they grow.

Opposite: Greater and Lesser flamingo stalk the alkaline waters of the Crater's Lake Makat (Magadi).

Above: Irate bull elephant stalks off after being disturbed by rubber-necking tourists.

But this book is deliberately short and time, to most of Ngorongoro's visitors, is limited, so that they spend their precious moments motoring from one area to another. This is quite natural and understandable and, in the circumstances, the best thing to do. But for those fortunate enough to have time to spare, there are few better ways of appreciating the splendour of the Crater than to drive, with your guide, to some secluded corner of the caldera, perhaps to one of the rocky outcrops where you can find strange, small depressions, regularly spaced in the lava.

These little hollows were man-made, no doubt gouged into the smooth lava by the pointed hafts of Maasai spears in bygone days, for the indentations, which here follow an eight-by-two format, make up the 'board' of a game which is popular among the Maasai and many other African tribes. It is known as 'Bau' (the Kiswahili word *mbau* for 'board', as the game is normally played on a wooden block). The number and arrangement of the depressions vary to some extent and the counters, usually pebbles, are placed in the hollows and moved around according to the rules of the game, which is said to be as complicated as chess.

Here, on such a raised outcrop, where history, impressive landscapes and skies and fascinating plants and animals come together, you will feel as well as see the beauty of Ngorongoro, and inherit, for all too brief a time, the enthralling kingdom by which you are encircled. Around you the Crater floor might be, if the cloud cover has lifted, a slowly moving mosaic of sunlight and cloud-shadow, perhaps with a brilliant tinge of greenness in the grass. And on this close-cropped sward might graze a scattering of zebra, or wildebeest, or gazelle.

Here, it is hoped, you will find the peace of mind that comes

with a sense of completeness, of being an integral part of a diverse and complex entirety. It is also hoped that this book has helped, in however small a way, to increase your enjoyment, and inspired you to find out more about Ngorongoro, and to make the most of every privileged moment within its boundaries, for those boundaries embrace — however wild and primitive it may be — a most intense and very special kind of beauty.

Overleaf: Afternoon sun over Lake Makat (Magadi).

Following pages: Sundown over Ngorongoro.
Pages 126-127: With the Crater wall in the background, flamingo, wildebeest,
rhino and zebra share the riches of Ngorongoro Crater.
Page 128: Lion cubs at rest in midday heat.